Ladybird I'm Ready... to Explore My World!

Written by Anita Ganeri
Illustrated by Barbara Bongini

Geography glossary

continent   Many countries together making up a very large area of land. There are seven different continents in the world.

country   An area of land where people live and are governed by the same rules. A country will have a leader like a president, prime minister, king or queen.

desert   A large area of hot, dry land with little plant or animal life, usually covered with sand.

ocean   Huge areas of cold salty water that cover over 70% of the Earth. There are five different oceans in the world.

sea   Large areas of salty water. These are smaller than oceans and can be divided into defined areas, such as the Mediterranean Sea.

volcano   An opening in the Earth's crust that usually looks like a mountain or hill. When they erupt they send out lava, gas, ash and hot rocks.

Geography consultant: Hannah Sassoon

LADYBIRD BOOKS

UK | USA | Canada | Ireland | Australia
India | New Zealand | South Africa

Ladybird Books is part of the Penguin Random House group of companies
whose addresses can be found at global.penguinrandomhouse.com.

ladybird.com

Penguin
Random House
UK

First published 2015

001

Copyright © Ladybird Books Ltd 2015

Printed in Hong Kong

A CIP catalogue record for this book is available from the British Library

ISBN: 978–0–723–29567–9

Contents

United Kingdom

My name is Lucy and I live in the United Kingdom. The UK is made up of four different countries: England, Wales, Scotland and Northern Ireland. Each has its own capital city.

Hello!

The flag of the UK is called the Union flag, or the Union Jack. It is a mix of the English, Scottish and Northern Irish flags.

Continent: Europe

Capital cities:

England: London
Scotland: Edinburgh
Wales: Cardiff
Northern Ireland: Belfast

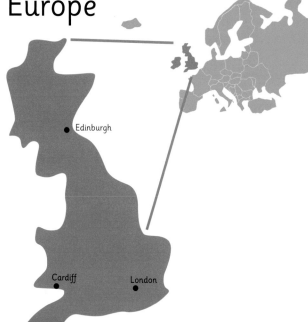

Edinburgh

Belfast

Cardiff

London

Main language spoken:

English

Buckingham Palace, in the centre of London, is the official home of the Queen. It has 775 rooms!

The highest mountain in Wales is Snowdon. You can climb to the top or go by train.

There are lots of large lakes in Scotland, called 'lochs'. Loch Ness is the deepest loch and has a famous story about its own monster!

The biggest tourist attraction in Northern Ireland is the Giant's Causeway, a natural rock formation.

DID YOU KNOW...?

In 2012, London was the first city to host the Olympic Games for a third time.

Over 700 islands are part of Scotland, including the Outer Hebrides and Shetland Islands.

France

My name is Stéphanie and I live in France.
As well as big cities such as Paris and Lyon,
France has both snowy mountains and sunny beaches.

Bonjour!

The flag of France is called the 'tricolore' (this means 'three colours').

Continent: Europe

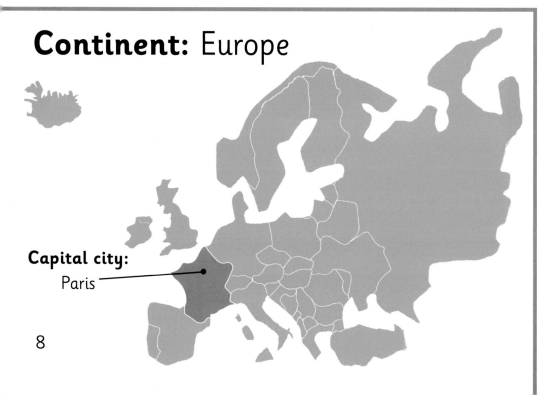

Capital city:
Paris

Main language spoken:

French

Mont Blanc is the highest mountain in France. It is in the Alps.

The Eiffel Tower in Paris was built in 1889. It is very heavy as it is made from 10,000 tonnes of metal.

The Tour de France is a famous cycle race. It takes place in July each year and the cyclists cover over 3,000 kilometres! It always finishes in Paris.

DID YOU KNOW...?

A popular French breakfast is hot chocolate drunk from a bowl. Sometimes bread is dipped into it, too.

The Louvre in Paris is one of the biggest art museums in the world. It used to be a royal palace.

My name is Manuel and I come from Spain. Spain has many beautiful sandy beaches and lots of sunshine, so many people like to visit on holiday.

¡Hola!

The flag is red and gold and has the Spanish royal coat of arms on it.

Continent: Europe

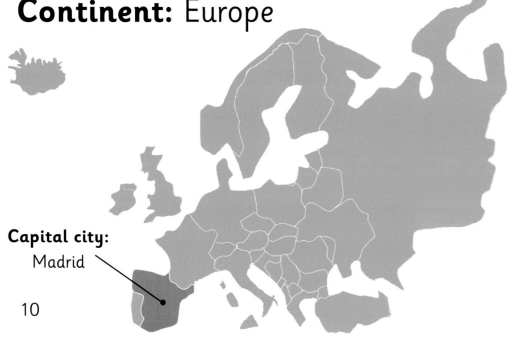

Capital city: Madrid

Main language spoken:

Spanish (also known as Castilian)

Spain

Flamenco is a lively Spanish dance with lots of stamping and whirling around.

In Spain, people often take a nap in the afternoon because it is so hot. This is called a 'siesta'.

Juicy oranges, grapes and olives are some of the foods that grow well in sunny Spain.

Paella is a tasty Spanish dish made with rice, fish, meat, tomatoes and peppers.

DID YOU KNOW...?

Instead of the tooth fairy, Spanish children leave their teeth for a mouse called Rantoncito Perez who gives them gifts.

Salvador Dalí is a famous artist who lived in Spain. He painted melting clocks and other strange scenes.

Poland

I am Piotr and I live in Poland. Poland has all sorts of landscapes including flat land that is good for farming and building cities. It also has forests, lakes and even mountain ranges in the south.

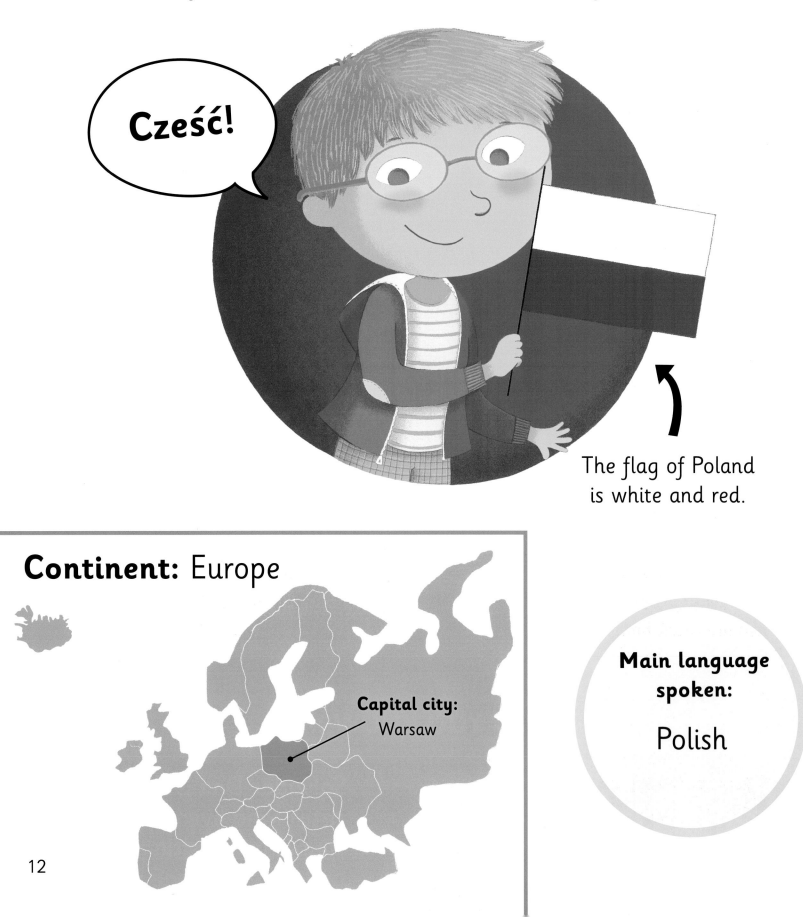

Cześć!

The flag of Poland is white and red.

Continent: Europe

Capital city: Warsaw

Main language spoken:

Polish

There are lots of farms in Poland. Farmers usually grow potatoes and sugar beet.

The longest river in Poland is called the Vistula. It is 1,047 kilometres long.

People like to eat bread rings called Obwarzanki. They are often bought from stalls in the street.

Hundreds of wild bison live in the many forests that cover Poland. Bison have long, shaggy fur.

DID YOU KNOW...?

The symbol of Poland is the white eagle.

Poland has over 1,300 lakes.

Norway

My name is Linnea and I live in Norway. Norway is famous for its amazing fjords, mountains and glaciers. Glaciers are areas of slow-moving thick ice that you can often ski or walk on.

Hei!

This is the flag of Norway. It is red with a blue and white cross.

Continent: Europe

Capital city:
Oslo

Main language spoken:

Norwegian

Fjords are long, thin valleys between steep cliffs.
There are hundreds along the Norwegian coast.

The Sami people live in the far north
of Norway. They keep herds of reindeer
and wear colourful clothing.

The Vikings lived in Norway
about 1,000 years ago.
They were warriors who travelled
great distances over the sea.

DID YOU KNOW...?

Some animals found in
Norway are polar foxes,
wolverines, seals, walruses,
moose and polar bears.

Norwegian children
don't start school until
they are seven years old.

Iceland

My name is Einar and I am from Iceland, an island in the far north of the Atlantic Ocean. Iceland has many volcanoes, waterfalls and geysers, which are jets of water that shoot up in the air.

Halló!

This is the flag of Iceland.
It is blue with a red and white cross.

Continent: Europe

Capital city:
Reykjavík

Main languages spoken:

Icelandic and English

Iceland

There are more than twenty active volcanoes in Iceland. In 2010, one erupted and caused an enormous ash cloud in the sky!

Iceland is a good place to spot the Northern Lights — swirling colours that can sometimes be seen in the night sky.

In winter, Iceland gets very cold. Even the waterfalls freeze solid.

Icelandic National Day is on 17 June. There is usually a parade and children are given sweets and balloons.

DID YOU KNOW...?

In summer, it never gets dark, even in the middle of the night.

One traditional Icelandic food is 'hákarl', which is rotting shark meat!

17

Turkey

My name is Bengisu and I come from Turkey.
Turkey has both vast deserts and big, bustling cities.
The highest mountain is called Mount Ararat.

Merhaba!

This is the flag of Turkey. It shows a crescent and a star.

Continent:
Europe and Asia

Capital city:
Ankara

Main language spoken:

Turkish

Turkish Delight is a yummy sugary sweet. Flavours include rose, pistachio and lemon.

Beautiful carpets are made in Turkey. They have bright colours and striking patterns and are often made by hand.

The city of Istanbul has many beautiful mosques. One of them is known as the Blue Mosque because the entire inside walls are decorated with blue tiles.

Turkish folk dances are often performed at events such as weddings and festivals. They tell a story through dance.

DID YOU KNOW...?

Istanbul is the only city in the world that is part of two continents. It is in both Asia and Europe.

In the region of Cappadocia you can find houses that have been carved out of rock.

Russia

I'm Sofiya and I come from Russia. Russia is part of both Europe and Asia. Although it is a very large country, it doesn't have the largest population. This is because most of Russia is a region called Siberia, which is too cold to live in.

Privyet!

This is the flag of Russia. It is white, blue and red.

Continent:
Europe and Asia

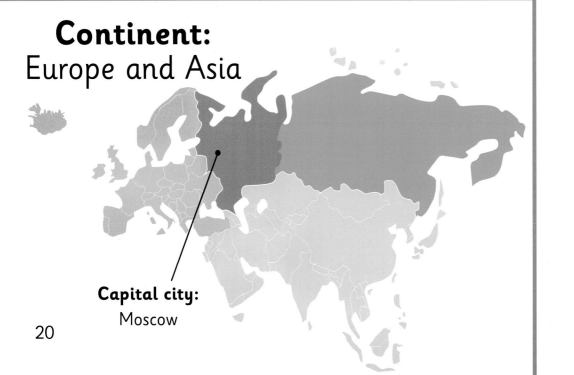

Capital city:
Moscow

Main language spoken:

Russian

Russia

Russian dolls are a famous souvenir.
They fit inside each other, in order of size.

To get from Moscow in the west
to the east coast of Russia by train
takes six days non-stop!

Lake Baikal in Siberia is the deepest
lake in the world.

Russians use a different alphabet.
The script is called 'Cyrillic'.

DID YOU KNOW...?

Russia is the biggest
country in the world. It is
also the widest country.

Russia has a lot of oil and gas
that is used around the world
for heating and electricity.

China

My name is Huan and I live in China. China has the largest population in the world – almost one in five people in the world are Chinese! Half of these people live in cities, which can be very crowded and busy.

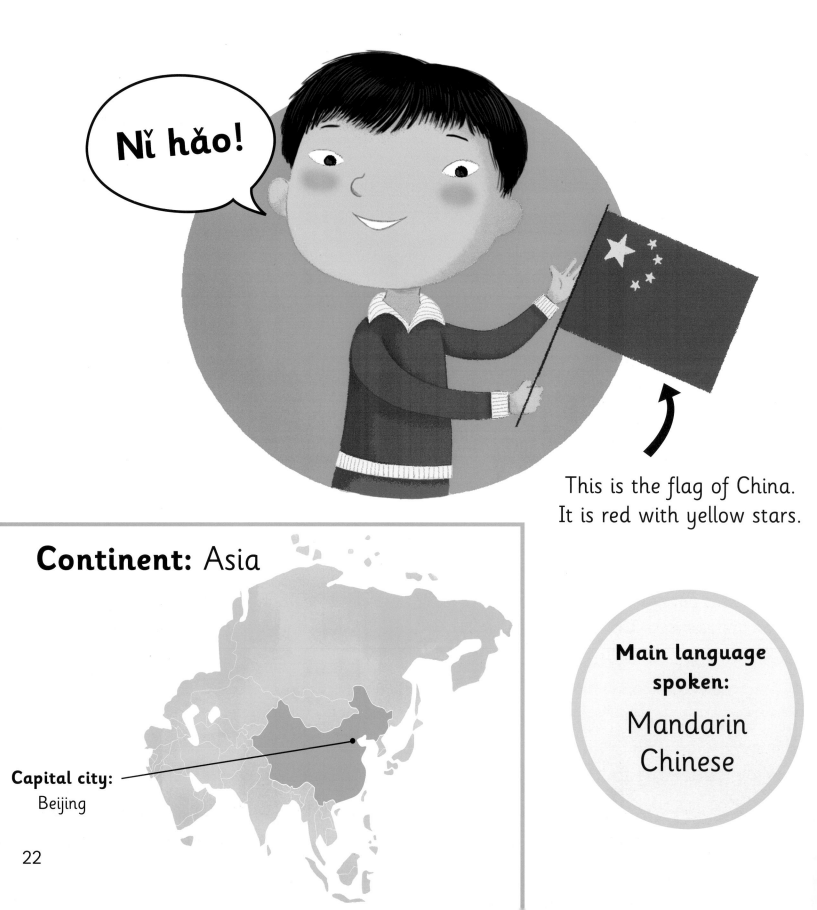

Nǐ hǎo!

This is the flag of China. It is red with yellow stars.

Continent: Asia

Capital city:
Beijing

Main language spoken:

Mandarin Chinese

China

The Great Wall of China was built hundreds of years ago and is the world's largest man-made structure. It is more than 21,000 kilometres long.

One of the main crops grown in China is rice. This is farmed in huge, wet fields called paddies.

Giant pandas live in the wild in some forests in China. They mostly eat a plant called bamboo.

In China, people often use wooden sticks called chopsticks to eat food instead of knives and forks.

DID YOU KNOW...?

The Yangtze is the longest river in China. It flows for more than 6,400 kilometres.

China has lots of factories that make goods such as clothes and electronics. These are shipped all over the world.

Japan

My name is Kumiko and I am from Japan. Japan is made up of four main islands – Honshu, Hokkaido, Shikoku and Kyushu. There are often earthquakes, so buildings are made to be very strong.

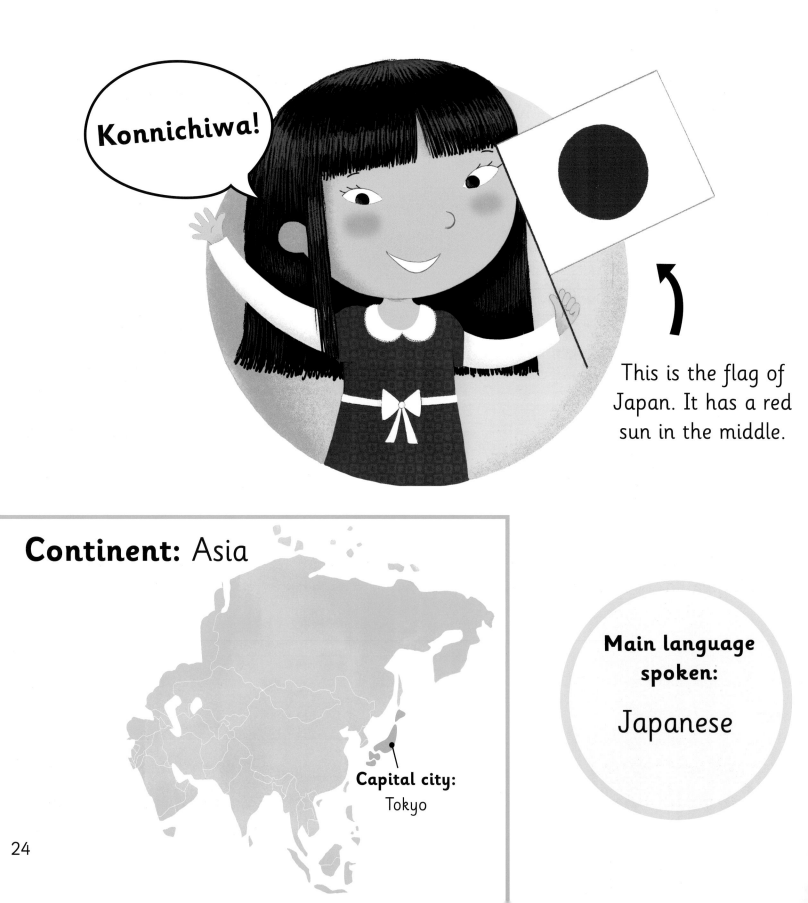

Konnichiwa!

This is the flag of Japan. It has a red sun in the middle.

Continent: Asia

Capital city:
Tokyo

Main language spoken:

Japanese

Japan

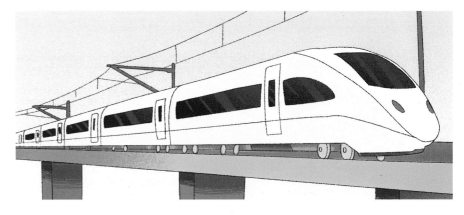

You can travel from one city to another by a super-fast bullet train.

Sushi is a popular Japanese food. This is made of raw fish with rice and seaweed and is eaten with chopsticks.

A type of traditional clothing for both men and women is a robe called a kimono.

Mount Fuji is a famous mountain in Japan. It is also a volcano.

DID YOU KNOW...?

When saying hello in Japan, people bow to each other to be polite.

The national sport is sumo wrestling, where two big men try and knock each other over.

India

I am Priya and I live in India. India is shaped like a triangle, with sea along the east and west coasts and mountains across the top. It often gets a lot of heavy rain, called a 'monsoon'.

Namaste!

This is the flag of India. It has a wheel in the middle that represents the Wheel of Law.

Continent: Asia

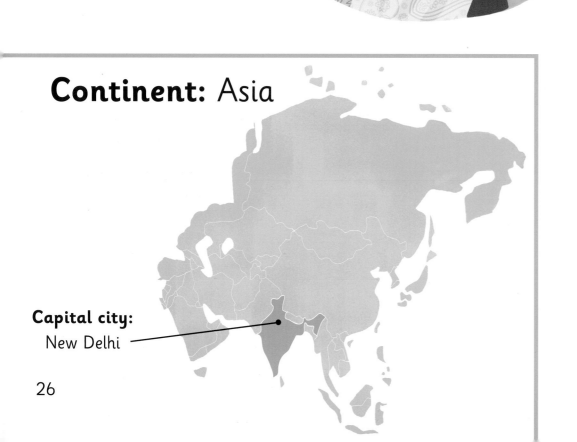

Capital city:
New Delhi

Main languages spoken:

Hindi, Bengali, and English

India

Women and girls often wear a sari. This is made from one long piece of material wrapped around the body.

Diwali is a festival of light. People light little clay lamps and give gifts. It is important for people who are Hindu or Sikh.

The Taj Mahal is a beautiful building in Agra, in North India. It is made from white marble.

Many Indian people are vegetarian, meaning they don't eat meat. Delicious meals often include rice, flatbread, vegetables, yoghurt and spices.

DID YOU KNOW...?

When you say 'Namaste', a traditional greeting, you press the palms of your hands together and bow your head slightly.

The most popular sport in India is cricket. It has been played there since 1848.

Australia

My name is Mia and I live in Australia. Australia is a large country that is all by itself in the ocean. The nearest country is Papua New Guinea, but it is still over 2,300 kilometres away!

G'day!

This is the flag of Australia. It has a small Union Jack and a pattern of stars.

Continent:
Australia

Capital city:
Canberra

Main language spoken:

English

Australia

The native Aboriginal people have lived in Australia for more than 50,000 years.

A large region of Australia is desert called the 'outback'. In the centre is a huge sandstone rock called Uluru.

Kangaroos, koalas and wombats are famous Australian animals.

The roof of the Sydney Opera House looks like the sails of a ship.

DID YOU KNOW...?

The Great Barrier Reef is the largest coral reef in the world and is home to many types of fish and sea creatures.

Australia is in the southern hemisphere. This means it is winter in July and summer in December.

I'm Justin. Welcome to the USA! The USA is divided into fifty areas called 'states' that together make up one country. This is why it is called the United States of America.

Hi!

The flag of the USA is called the 'Stars and Stripes'. The stars on the flag represent all the different states.

Continent: North America

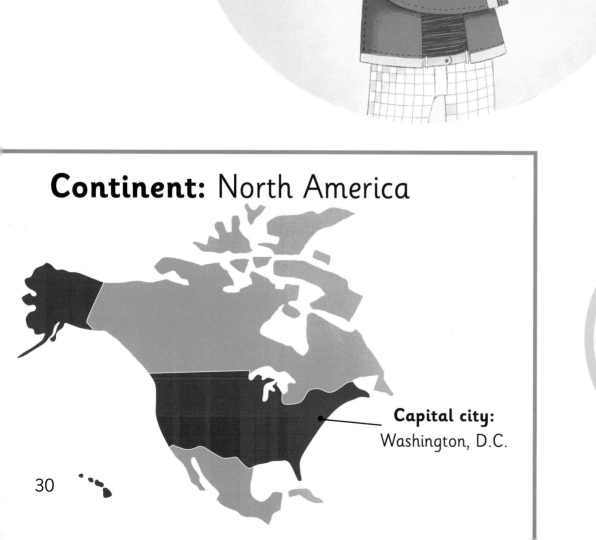

Capital city:
Washington, D.C.

Main language spoken:

English

Hollywood is a part of Los Angeles and is a famous area for making films. Lots of film stars live there.

Sometimes, tornadoes hit the USA. Tornadoes are giant, spinning storms and can cause a lot of damage.

Baseball is the national sport of the USA. It is played by two teams of nine players.

The Empire State Building in New York City is a famous skyscraper. It is 103 floors high.

DID YOU KNOW...?

One of the states of the USA is actually a group of islands in the Pacific Ocean called Hawaii.

Silicon Valley is an area where lots of computer and phone technology has been invented.

Canada

I'm Sophie and I live in Canada. Huge forests grow here and there are lots of lakes and mountains. It can also be very cold so not many people live in the freezing north of the country.

The Canadian flag has a red maple leaf in the middle. This is the symbol of Canada.

Continent: North America

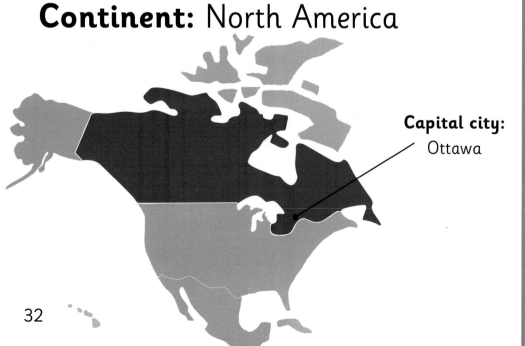

Capital city:
Ottawa

Main languages spoken:

English and French

A small group of people called the Inuit live in the far north. They speak a language called Inuktitut.

Canada is famous for sweet maple syrup that comes from maple trees.

Niagara Falls is between Canada and the USA and is made up of three waterfalls: the American Falls, the Bridal Veil Falls and the Horseshoe Falls.

The CN Tower in Toronto is 553 metres tall and one of the tallest towers in the world.

DID YOU KNOW...?

In the region called Québec, people speak a type of French called Québécois.

The national winter sport of Canada is ice hockey.

I am Santiago and I live in Mexico. Mexico is a warm and sunny country with both deserts and rainforests. It is also home to lots of different animals and plants.

¡Hola!

This is the flag of Mexico. It has an eagle, a snake and a cactus on it.

Continent: North America

Capital city:
Mexico City

Main language spoken:

Spanish

The Day of the Dead is a holiday where people dress up as skeletons and buy sugar skulls. It is a way of honouring dead loved ones.

Long ago, people called the Aztecs lived in Mexico. They left many amazing old buildings behind.

Lizards like this one live in the Sonora Desert. There are giant prickly cacti, too.

Popocatépetl is an active volcano near Mexico City. Its name is the Aztec word for 'smoking mountain'.

DID YOU KNOW...?

One delicious Mexican food is the taco. It is a thin pancake filled with meat and vegetables.

The most popular sport in Mexico is football.

My name is Patrick and I live in Jamaica. Jamaica is an island in the Caribbean Sea that is warm and sunny with beautiful beaches.

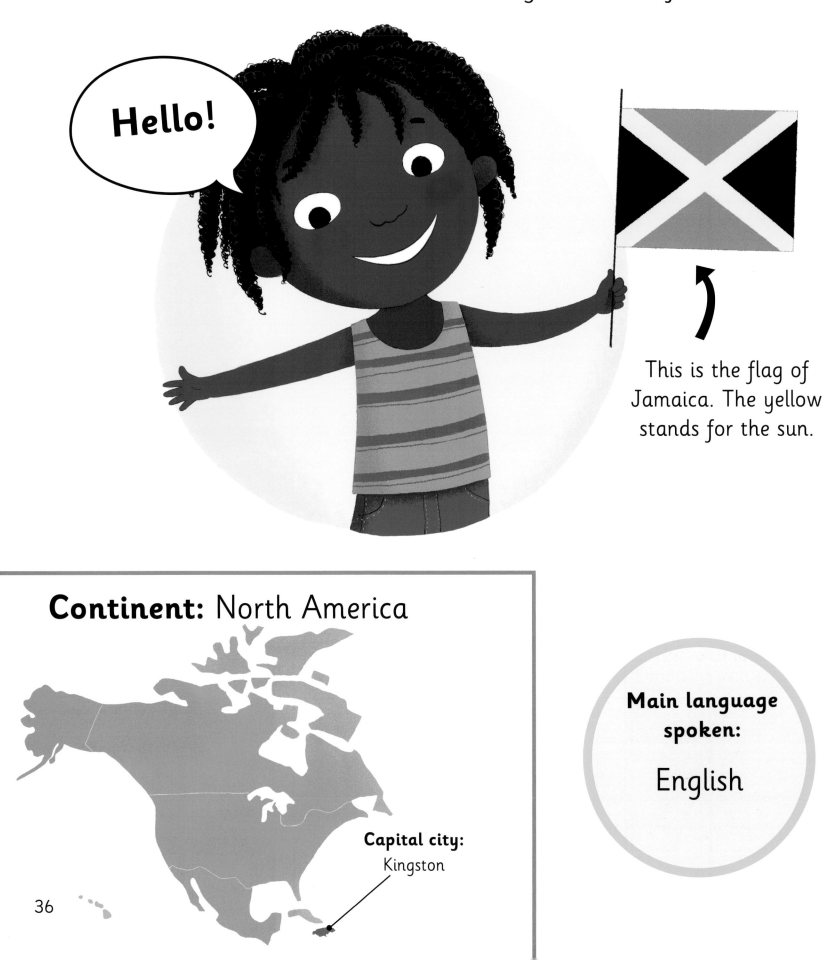

Hello!

This is the flag of Jamaica. The yellow stands for the sun.

Continent: North America

Main language spoken:

English

Capital city:
Kingston

36

Jamaica

Lots of fruit grows on the island, and the national fruit is ackee. Ackee is often eaten with fish.

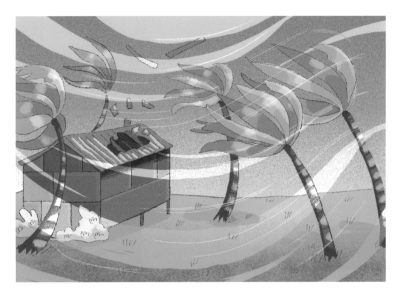

Fierce storms called hurricanes often hit Jamaica. They can do a lot of damage.

The nation's favourite sport is cricket, but football and athletics are also popular.

Jamaica is famous for inventing reggae music. It's great for dancing to.

DID YOU KNOW...?

Jamaica is home to the Giant Swallowtail butterfly. Its wingspan can be 25 centimetres.

Jamaica has competed in two Winter Olympics despite not having any snow!

My name is Rosa and I come from Brazil. Brazil is the largest country in South America and the only one where Portuguese is spoken. It is famous for its beautiful beaches and the amazing Amazon rainforest.

Olá!

This is the flag of Brazil. It shows the stars in the sky at night.

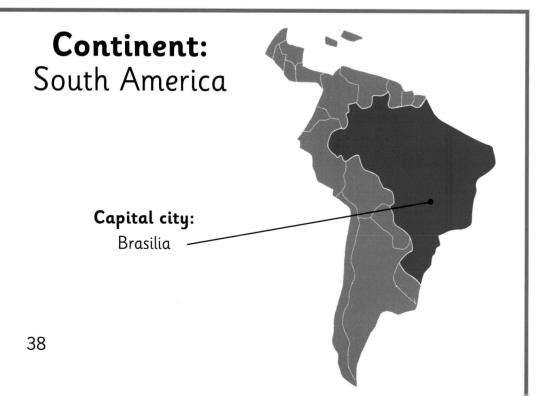

Continent:
South America

Capital city:
Brasilia

Main language spoken:
Brazilian Portuguese

Brazil

The Amazon River flows 6,400 kilometres through Brazil from the mountains to the sea.

This is a huge statue called Christ the Redeemer. It stands on a hill outside the city of Rio de Janeiro.

The Amazon Rainforest is the largest rainforest in the world. It is home to many different birds, animals and plants.

Brazilians love to celebrate Carnival every year. This is a celebration where people dress up in colourful costumes and masks and dance in the streets.

DID YOU KNOW...?

Brazil is the only country to have won the football World Cup five times.

Some Amazonian tribes live deep in the rainforest and have no contact at all with the rest of the world.

Welcome to Egypt. My name is Jamila. Egypt is a very dry, hot country that is well-known for its Ancient Egyptian ancient civilization. It is a very popular place to go on holiday as it is warm all year.

Ahlan!

This is the flag of Egypt. It has an eagle in the middle.

Continent:
Africa

Capital city:
Cairo

Main language spoken:

Arabic

The Sahara desert covers most of North Africa. It is very hot and sandy. The Bedouin are desert people who move from place to place. This is easy for them as they live in tents.

Egypt is famous for its pyramids. They were built thousands of years ago by the Ancient Egyptians.

The Nile is the longest river in the world. The land surrounding the Nile is good for farming and building on.

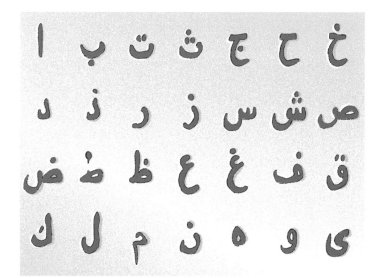

Arabic is written in a special script. Unlike English, it is read from right to left.

DID YOU KNOW...?

Cairo has been a city for over 6,000 years. It is also the largest capital city in Africa.

A popular Egyptian snack is pitta bread and falafel. Falafel are balls of mashed-up chickpeas.

Nigeria

Hello, I am Adebayo and I come from Nigeria. Nigeria is a country in the west of Africa. Most of the land is made up of grassy plains but there are also jungles, swamps and mountains.

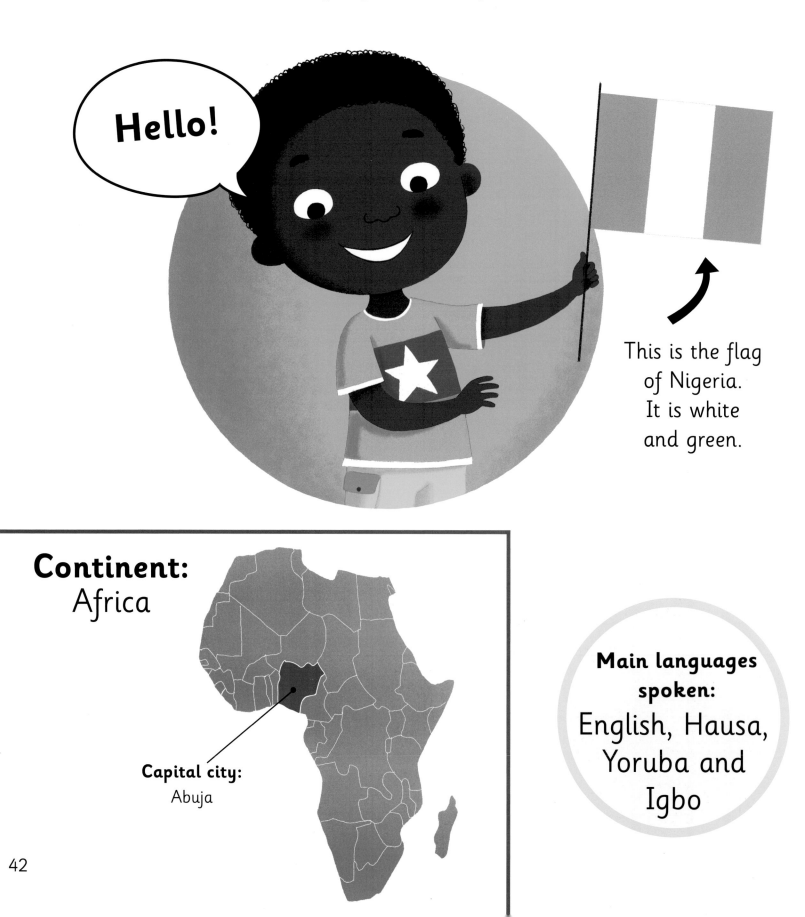

Hello!

This is the flag of Nigeria. It is white and green.

Continent:
Africa

Capital city:
Abuja

Main languages spoken:
English, Hausa, Yoruba and Igbo

Nigeria

The Niger River is more than 4,000 kilometres long. It flows through Nigeria and empties into the Atlantic Ocean.

Many Nigerians love football. The Nigerian team is called the Super Eagles.

Farmers grow lots of palm nuts, groundnuts and cocoa.

The Yoruba people have lived in Nigeria for thousands of years. They play lively music on the drums.

DID YOU KNOW...?

Nigeria has the largest population of all African countries.

There are over 500 different languages spoken throughout the country.

South Africa

I'm Kwanele and I live in South Africa.
South Africa is a country with many beautiful things to see, such as wildlife reserves, mountains, beaches and waterfalls.

Hallo!

This is the flag of South Africa. Each colour represents different parts of the country.

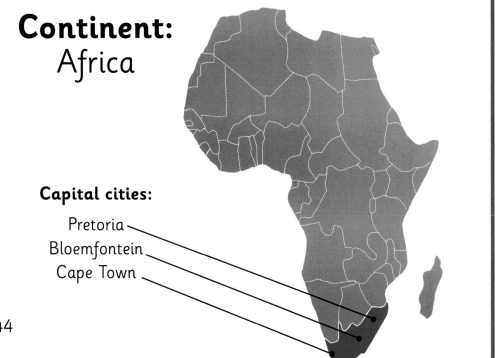

Continent:
Africa

Capital cities:

Pretoria
Bloemfontein
Cape Town

Main languages spoken:
English and Afrikaans

The Zulu people are known for their war dances. They stamp their feet hard on the ground to show their strength.

The Kruger National Park is a great place for seeing elephants, giraffes and zebras.

This is Table Mountain near Cape Town. It has a flat top like a table.

Johannesburg is the biggest city in South Africa. About 4 million people live there.

DID YOU KNOW...?

There are eleven official languages in South Africa, including English, Afrikaans, Zulu and Xhosa.

Some of the world's fastest land animals live in South Africa – the cheetah, the wildebeest and the lion.

Canada

NORTH AMERICA

USA

Mexico

Jamaica

Iceland

ATLANTIC OCEAN

PACIFIC OCEAN

Brazil

SOUTH AMERICA

N

W

E

S